45 Christmas
Recipes for Home

By: Kelly Johnson

Table of Contents

Appetizers:

- Holiday Cheese Ball Bites
- Cranberry Brie Crostini
- Shrimp Cocktail Christmas Tree
- Spinach and Artichoke Stuffed Mushrooms
- Festive Caprese Skewers
- Prosciutto-Wrapped Asparagus
- Cranberry Pecan Goat Cheese Bites
- Festive Stuffed Mushrooms
- Smoked Salmon Canapés

Mains:

- Roast Turkey with Cranberry Glaze
- Honey Glazed Ham
- Herb-Crusted Prime Rib
- Maple Dijon Glazed Salmon
- Vegetarian Wellington
- Stuffed Acorn Squash with White Rice and Cranberries
- Beef Wellington
- Herb-Roasted Chicken with Citrus Glaze
- Pomegranate Glazed Pork Tenderloin
- Vegetarian Stuffed Bell Peppers

Sides:

- Garlic Mashed Potatoes
- Roasted Brussel Sprouts with Balsamic Glaze
- Cranberry Orange Quinoa Salad
- Creamy Green Bean Casserole
- Sweet Potato Casserole with Pecan Streusel
- Butternut Squash and Sage Risotto
- Cranberry Walnut Stuffing
- Maple Glazed Carrots

- Creamed Corn Casserole
- Hasselback Potatoes with Rosemary and Garlic

Desserts:

- Classic Christmas Cookies (Sugar, Gingerbread, Peppermint)
- Yule Log Cake (Bûche de Noël)
- Eggnog Cheesecake
- Peppermint Bark
- Pecan Pie Bars

Drinks:

- Spiced Mulled Wine
- Holiday Punch
- Peppermint White Hot Chocolate
- Cranberry Orange Sangria
- Homemade Eggnog

Breakfast/Brunch:

- Christmas Morning Casserole
- Gingerbread Pancakes
- Cranberry Orange Scones
- Overnight Cinnamon Rolls
- Eggnog French Toast Bake

Appetizers:

Holiday Cheese Ball Bites

Ingredients:

- 8 ounces cream cheese, softened
- 1 1/2 cups shredded sharp cheddar cheese
- 1/2 cup crumbled feta cheese
- 1/4 cup finely chopped green onions
- 1/4 cup finely chopped fresh parsley
- 1/4 teaspoon garlic powder
- 1/4 teaspoon onion powder
- 1/4 teaspoon dried dill
- 1/4 teaspoon black pepper
- 1 cup finely chopped nuts (pecans or almonds work well)
- 1/2 cup dried cranberries, finely chopped
- Pretzel sticks or sturdy crackers for serving

Instructions:

In a large bowl, combine the softened cream cheese, shredded cheddar, crumbled feta, green onions, parsley, garlic powder, onion powder, dill, and black pepper. Mix until well combined.
Shape the mixture into bite-sized balls, about 1 inch in diameter. Place the balls on a parchment-lined tray and refrigerate for at least 30 minutes to firm up.
In a shallow dish, combine the finely chopped nuts and dried cranberries.
Roll each cheese ball in the nut and cranberry mixture, pressing lightly to coat the entire surface.
Once all the cheese balls are coated, return them to the refrigerator for another 30 minutes or until ready to serve.
Just before serving, insert a pretzel stick into each cheese ball to create a bite-sized appetizer.
Arrange the Holiday Cheese Ball Bites on a festive serving platter and enjoy!

These little bites are not only delicious but also visually appealing, making them a perfect addition to your holiday spread. Feel free to customize the recipe by adding your favorite herbs, spices, or coatings.

Cranberry Brie Crostini

Ingredients:

- Baguette, thinly sliced
- 1 wheel of Brie cheese, sliced
- 1 cup cranberry sauce (homemade or store-bought)
- Fresh rosemary, for garnish (optional)

Instructions:

Preheat your oven to 375°F (190°C).
Arrange the baguette slices on a baking sheet. You can brush them lightly with olive oil for added flavor, if desired.
Toast the baguette slices in the preheated oven for about 5-7 minutes or until they are golden and crispy. Keep an eye on them to prevent burning.
While the crostini is toasting, heat the cranberry sauce in a small saucepan over low heat. You can add a splash of water to loosen it if needed. Stir occasionally until it reaches a spreadable consistency.
Once the crostini is toasted, remove them from the oven and let them cool for a minute or two.
Place a slice of Brie cheese on each crostini.
Spoon a small amount of warm cranberry sauce on top of the Brie.
If desired, garnish each crostini with a small sprig of fresh rosemary for added flavor and a festive touch.
Serve the Cranberry Brie Crostini on a platter and enjoy!

This appetizer is perfect for holiday gatherings or any occasion where you want to impress your guests with a tasty and visually appealing dish. Adjust the quantities based on the number of guests you're serving.

Shrimp Cocktail Christmas Tree

Ingredients:

- Cooked shrimp (peeled and deveined)
- Cocktail sauce
- Fresh parsley or dill (for decoration)
- Lemon wedges (optional, for garnish)

Instructions:

Prepare the Shrimp:
- Ensure the shrimp are fully cooked, peeled, and deveined.
- You can leave the tails on for a decorative touch, or remove them for easier eating.

Create the Tree Base:
- Choose a large serving platter or board to build your tree on.
- Start arranging the shrimp in the shape of a Christmas tree. Place the larger shrimp at the bottom and gradually use smaller shrimp as you move upward.

Prepare the Cocktail Sauce:
- Place cocktail sauce in a bowl and set it at the base of the tree, shaping it like a tree trunk.

Decorate with Fresh Herbs:
- Use fresh parsley or dill sprigs to create the appearance of tree branches. Arrange them between the layers of shrimp.

Garnish with Lemon Wedges:
- Optionally, garnish the platter with lemon wedges for a pop of color and to add a citrusy element to the dish.

Additional Decoration (Optional):
- If you want to add more festive elements, consider using small cherry tomatoes as ornaments or small pieces of red pepper for a decorative touch.

Chill Before Serving:
- Place the Shrimp Cocktail Christmas Tree in the refrigerator for a short time before serving to ensure the shrimp stay cool.

Serve and Enjoy:

- Present your Shrimp Cocktail Christmas Tree to your guests as a stunning and tasty centerpiece. Provide small bowls for dipping in the cocktail sauce.

This creative and edible holiday decoration is sure to be a hit at your Christmas gathering. Feel free to customize it based on your preferences and the size of your guest list.

Spinach and Artichoke Stuffed Mushrooms

Ingredients:

- 24 large button mushrooms, cleaned and stems removed
- 1 tablespoon olive oil
- 1 small onion, finely chopped
- 2 cloves garlic, minced
- 1 cup fresh spinach, chopped
- 1 (14-ounce) can artichoke hearts, drained and chopped
- 1/2 cup cream cheese, softened
- 1/2 cup mayonnaise
- 1/2 cup grated Parmesan cheese
- Salt and pepper to taste
- 1/2 cup shredded mozzarella cheese (optional, for topping)
- Fresh parsley, chopped, for garnish

Instructions:

Preheat the oven to 375°F (190°C).
Clean the mushrooms and remove the stems. Place the mushroom caps on a baking sheet lined with parchment paper.
In a skillet, heat olive oil over medium heat. Add chopped onions and garlic, sauté until softened.
Add chopped spinach to the skillet and cook until wilted. Stir in the chopped artichoke hearts and cook for an additional 2-3 minutes. Remove from heat.
In a mixing bowl, combine the cream cheese, mayonnaise, grated Parmesan cheese, and the sautéed spinach-artichoke mixture. Mix until well combined. Season with salt and pepper to taste.
Spoon the spinach and artichoke filling into the mushroom caps, mounding it slightly.
If desired, sprinkle shredded mozzarella cheese on top of each stuffed mushroom.
Bake in the preheated oven for about 15-20 minutes, or until the mushrooms are tender and the filling is hot and bubbly.
Remove from the oven and garnish with chopped fresh parsley.
Allow the stuffed mushrooms to cool slightly before serving.

These Spinach and Artichoke Stuffed Mushrooms are a crowd-pleaser and perfect for any gathering or party. The combination of spinach, artichoke, and cheesy goodness in each bite is sure to be a hit!

Festive Caprese Skewers

Ingredients:

- Cherry tomatoes
- Fresh mozzarella balls (bocconcini)
- Fresh basil leaves
- Balsamic glaze or balsamic reduction
- Extra virgin olive oil
- Salt and pepper, to taste
- Wooden skewers or toothpicks

Instructions:

Prepare the Ingredients:
- Wash the cherry tomatoes and basil leaves.
- Drain the fresh mozzarella balls if they are stored in water.

Assemble the Skewers:
- Take a wooden skewer or toothpick and thread on one cherry tomato, followed by a fresh basil leaf (folded if large), and then a mozzarella ball.
- Repeat the process until you have a desired number of skewers.

Arrange on a Platter:
- Place the assembled skewers on a serving platter.

Season and Drizzle:
- Drizzle the skewers with extra virgin olive oil and balsamic glaze or balsamic reduction.
- Season with a pinch of salt and pepper to taste.

Serve and Enjoy:
- Arrange the Festive Caprese Skewers on a platter and serve immediately.

The combination of sweet cherry tomatoes, creamy mozzarella, and fragrant basil drizzled with balsamic glaze creates a burst of flavor in each bite. These skewers not only taste great but also add a colorful and festive touch to your appetizer spread. They are perfect for holiday gatherings, parties, or any occasion where you want a fresh and light appetizer.

Prosciutto-Wrapped Asparagus

Ingredients:

- Fresh asparagus spears, woody ends trimmed
- Prosciutto slices (1 slice for every 2-3 asparagus spears)
- Olive oil
- Black pepper, freshly ground
- Balsamic glaze (optional, for drizzling)

Instructions:

Preheat the Oven:
- Preheat your oven to 400°F (200°C).

Prepare the Asparagus:
- Trim the woody ends from the asparagus spears. If the spears are thick, you may want to peel the lower part of the stalks with a vegetable peeler.

Wrap with Prosciutto:
- Take a slice of prosciutto and wrap it around 2-3 asparagus spears, depending on the size.

Place on Baking Sheet:
- Arrange the prosciutto-wrapped asparagus on a baking sheet lined with parchment paper, making sure they are not too crowded.

Drizzle with Olive Oil:
- Lightly drizzle olive oil over the prosciutto-wrapped asparagus. This helps crisp up the prosciutto during baking.

Season with Black Pepper:
- Sprinkle freshly ground black pepper over the asparagus for added flavor.

Bake in the Oven:
- Bake in the preheated oven for about 10-15 minutes or until the asparagus is tender, and the prosciutto is crispy.

Optional Balsamic Glaze:
- If desired, drizzle the baked prosciutto-wrapped asparagus with balsamic glaze just before serving.

Serve Warm:
- Arrange the Prosciutto-Wrapped Asparagus on a serving platter and serve warm.

This appetizer is not only delicious but also visually appealing, making it a perfect addition to your appetizer spread, especially during special occasions or gatherings. The combination of the salty prosciutto and the tender-crisp asparagus is sure to be a crowd-pleaser.

Cranberry Pecan Goat Cheese Bites

Ingredients:

- 4 ounces goat cheese, softened
- 1/4 cup dried cranberries, finely chopped
- 1/4 cup pecans, finely chopped
- 1 tablespoon honey
- Crackers or baguette slices for serving

Instructions:

Prepare the Goat Cheese Mixture:
- In a bowl, mix the softened goat cheese, finely chopped dried cranberries, and finely chopped pecans until well combined.

Form Bite-Sized Balls:
- Take small portions of the goat cheese mixture and roll them into bite-sized balls.

Drizzle with Honey:
- Arrange the goat cheese balls on a serving platter and drizzle them with honey.

Chill:
- Place the platter in the refrigerator for at least 30 minutes to allow the flavors to meld and the cheese to firm up slightly.

Serve:
- Just before serving, arrange the Cranberry Pecan Goat Cheese Bites on crackers or baguette slices.

Garnish (Optional):
- Optionally, you can garnish each bite with a small additional sprinkle of finely chopped cranberries and pecans for added texture and visual appeal.

Serve and Enjoy:
- Serve these delightful bites at room temperature and enjoy the creamy, tangy, sweet, and nutty flavors in each bite.

Cranberry Pecan Goat Cheese Bites are perfect for holiday gatherings, cocktail parties, or any occasion where you want to impress your guests with a delicious and elegant appetizer. The combination of flavors and textures makes these bites a crowd-pleaser.

Festive Stuffed Mushrooms

Ingredients:

- 24 large button mushrooms, cleaned and stems removed
- 1 tablespoon olive oil
- 1 small onion, finely chopped
- 2 cloves garlic, minced
- 1/2 cup breadcrumbs
- 1/4 cup grated Parmesan cheese
- 1/4 cup chopped fresh parsley
- 1/4 cup dried cranberries, finely chopped
- 1/4 cup chopped pecans or walnuts (optional)
- Salt and pepper, to taste
- 1/4 cup melted butter
- Additional grated Parmesan for topping

Instructions:

Preheat the Oven:
- Preheat your oven to 375°F (190°C).

Prepare the Mushrooms:
- Clean the mushrooms and remove the stems. Place the mushroom caps on a baking sheet.

Prepare the Filling:
- In a skillet, heat olive oil over medium heat. Add chopped onions and garlic, sauté until softened.
- Add breadcrumbs to the skillet and toast until golden brown. Remove from heat.
- In a mixing bowl, combine the toasted breadcrumb mixture, grated Parmesan, chopped fresh parsley, dried cranberries, chopped nuts (if using), salt, and pepper. Mix well.
- Spoon the filling into the mushroom caps, pressing down gently.
- Drizzle melted butter over the stuffed mushrooms.
- Sprinkle additional grated Parmesan on top for added flavor.
- Bake in the preheated oven for approximately 15-20 minutes or until the mushrooms are tender and the filling is golden brown.
- Remove from the oven and let them cool slightly before serving.

These Festive Stuffed Mushrooms are savory, slightly sweet, and crunchy, making them a perfect addition to your holiday appetizer spread. Adjust the ingredients according to your preferences and enjoy these flavorful bites at your festive gatherings.

Smoked Salmon Canapés

Ingredients:

- 1 French baguette, thinly sliced
- 8 ounces (about 225g) smoked salmon, thinly sliced
- 1/2 cup cream cheese, softened
- 2 tablespoons fresh dill, chopped
- 1 tablespoon capers, drained
- 1 tablespoon red onion, finely diced
- Lemon wedges for garnish
- Freshly ground black pepper

Instructions:

Prepare the Baguette Slices:
- Preheat your oven to 375°F (190°C).
- Arrange the thinly sliced baguette on a baking sheet and toast in the oven until golden brown. Keep an eye on them to prevent burning. Alternatively, you can brush the slices with olive oil before toasting for added flavor.

Prepare the Cream Cheese Mixture:
- In a bowl, mix the softened cream cheese with chopped fresh dill.

Assemble the Canapés:
- Spread a thin layer of the dill cream cheese onto each toasted baguette slice.
- Place a slice of smoked salmon on top of the cream cheese layer.
- Garnish each canapé with a few capers, finely diced red onion, and a sprinkle of freshly ground black pepper.

Serve and Garnish:
- Arrange the Smoked Salmon Canapés on a serving platter.
- Garnish with additional fresh dill and lemon wedges.

Serve and Enjoy:
- Serve these delicious canapés immediately. The combination of smoked salmon, creamy dill cheese, and tangy capers creates a flavorful and visually appealing appetizer.

These Smoked Salmon Canapés are not only tasty but also easy to prepare, making them a perfect choice for entertaining guests. Adjust the quantities based on the number of guests you're serving.

Mains:
Roast Turkey with Cranberry Glaze

Ingredients:

- 1 whole turkey (12-15 pounds)
- Salt and pepper, to taste
- 1 cup unsalted butter, melted
- 1 cup cranberry sauce (homemade or store-bought)
- 1/2 cup orange juice
- 1/4 cup honey
- 2 tablespoons Dijon mustard
- 1 teaspoon dried thyme
- 1 teaspoon dried rosemary
- 1 teaspoon garlic powder
- 1 teaspoon onion powder
- Fresh cranberries and fresh herbs (rosemary and thyme) for garnish (optional)

Instructions:

Preheat the Oven:
- Preheat your oven to 325°F (163°C).

Prepare the Turkey:
- Remove the giblets and neck from the turkey cavity. Rinse the turkey under cold water and pat it dry with paper towels.
- Season the turkey inside and out with salt and pepper.

Make the Cranberry Glaze:
- In a saucepan over medium heat, combine melted butter, cranberry sauce, orange juice, honey, Dijon mustard, dried thyme, dried rosemary, garlic powder, and onion powder. Stir until well combined and the cranberry sauce is melted. Remove from heat.

Baste the Turkey:
- Place the seasoned turkey on a roasting rack in a large roasting pan.
- Brush the turkey generously with the cranberry glaze, reserving some for basting during cooking.

Roast the Turkey:
- Roast the turkey in the preheated oven, basting every 30 minutes with the cranberry glaze.

- Roast until the internal temperature of the turkey thigh reaches 165°F (74°C). Cooking time will vary based on the size of the turkey; plan for approximately 15 minutes per pound.

Rest and Garnish:
- Once the turkey is done, tent it with foil and let it rest for at least 20-30 minutes before carving.
- Garnish with fresh cranberries and herbs if desired.

Carve and Serve:
- Carve the turkey and serve with the remaining cranberry glaze on the side.

This Roast Turkey with Cranberry Glaze will add a festive and flavorful touch to your holiday table. The cranberry glaze not only enhances the flavor but also gives the turkey a beautiful, glossy appearance. Enjoy!

Honey Glazed Ham

Ingredients:

- 1 bone-in fully cooked ham (7-9 pounds)
- 1 cup honey
- 1/2 cup brown sugar, packed
- 1/4 cup Dijon mustard
- 2 tablespoons apple cider vinegar
- Whole cloves for garnish (optional)
- Pineapple rings and maraschino cherries for decoration (optional)

Instructions:

Preheat the Oven:
- Preheat your oven to 325°F (163°C).

Prepare the Ham:
- If the ham comes with a rind, remove it, leaving a thin layer of fat. Score the fat in a diamond pattern with a sharp knife.

Mix the Glaze:
- In a small saucepan, combine honey, brown sugar, Dijon mustard, and apple cider vinegar. Heat over medium heat, stirring, until the sugar is dissolved. Remove from heat.

Glaze the Ham:
- Place the ham on a rack in a roasting pan, fat side up. Brush the ham with a generous amount of the honey glaze, ensuring it gets into the scored lines.

Bake the Ham:
- Bake the ham in the preheated oven, uncovered, for about 1.5 to 2 hours or until the internal temperature reaches at least 140°F (60°C). Baste the ham with the honey glaze every 30 minutes.

Garnish (Optional):
- If desired, stud the scored intersections with whole cloves for added flavor. Decorate the ham with pineapple rings and maraschino cherries during the last 30 minutes of baking.

Rest and Carve:
- Once done, remove the ham from the oven and let it rest for about 15-20 minutes before carving.

Slice and Serve:
- Carve the ham into slices and serve with the remaining honey glaze as a sauce on the side.

This Honey Glazed Ham is a flavorful and impressive centerpiece for any holiday or special occasion. The combination of honey, brown sugar, and mustard creates a sweet and savory glaze that enhances the natural richness of the ham. Enjoy!

Herb-Crusted Prime Rib

Ingredients:

- 1 bone-in prime rib roast (about 4-5 pounds)
- Salt and black pepper, to taste
- 4 cloves garlic, minced
- 2 tablespoons Dijon mustard
- 2 tablespoons fresh rosemary, finely chopped
- 2 tablespoons fresh thyme, finely chopped
- 2 tablespoons fresh parsley, finely chopped
- 2 tablespoons olive oil
- 1 cup beef broth

Instructions:

Preheat the Oven:
- Preheat your oven to 450°F (232°C).

Prepare the Prime Rib:
- Make sure the prime rib is at room temperature. Pat it dry with paper towels.
- Season the roast generously with salt and black pepper.

Make the Herb Crust:
- In a bowl, mix together minced garlic, Dijon mustard, chopped rosemary, thyme, parsley, and olive oil to form a paste.

Apply the Herb Crust:
- Spread the herb paste evenly over the entire surface of the prime rib.

Roast the Prime Rib:
- Place the prime rib on a rack in a roasting pan, rib side down. Roast in the preheated oven for 15 minutes to sear the meat.
- After the initial searing, reduce the oven temperature to 325°F (163°C) and continue roasting for about 1.5 to 2 hours, or until the internal temperature reaches your desired doneness (use a meat thermometer for accuracy).

Rest the Prime Rib:
- Once the prime rib reaches the desired doneness, remove it from the oven and transfer it to a cutting board. Tent it with foil and let it rest for at least 15-20 minutes.

Make Au Jus:

- While the prime rib is resting, make a simple au jus by deglazing the roasting pan with beef broth over medium heat. Strain the liquid and serve as a sauce.

Slice and Serve:
- Carve the prime rib into slices and serve with the au jus on the side.

This Herb-Crusted Prime Rib is sure to impress your guests with its flavorful herb crust and juicy, tender interior. Adjust the cooking time based on the size of your prime rib and your preferred level of doneness.

Maple Dijon Glazed Salmon

Ingredients:

- 4 salmon fillets (about 6 ounces each)
- Salt and black pepper, to taste
- 2 tablespoons Dijon mustard
- 2 tablespoons pure maple syrup
- 1 tablespoon soy sauce
- 1 tablespoon olive oil
- 2 cloves garlic, minced
- 1 teaspoon fresh ginger, grated (optional)
- Fresh parsley or green onions, chopped, for garnish

Instructions:

Preheat the Oven:
- Preheat your oven to 400°F (200°C).

Prepare the Salmon:
- Place the salmon fillets on a baking sheet lined with parchment paper. Season each fillet with salt and black pepper.

Make the Maple Dijon Glaze:
- In a small bowl, whisk together Dijon mustard, maple syrup, soy sauce, olive oil, minced garlic, and grated ginger (if using).

Brush the Salmon:
- Brush the salmon fillets generously with the maple Dijon glaze, making sure to coat them evenly.

Bake the Salmon:
- Bake the salmon in the preheated oven for about 12-15 minutes or until the salmon is cooked through and easily flakes with a fork. Cooking time may vary based on the thickness of your salmon fillets.

Broil for Caramelization (Optional):
- If you want a caramelized finish, you can broil the salmon for an additional 2-3 minutes at the end of the cooking time. Keep a close eye to prevent burning.

Garnish and Serve:
- Remove the salmon from the oven, garnish with chopped fresh parsley or green onions, and serve immediately.

This Maple Dijon Glazed Salmon is a quick and flavorful dish that's perfect for a weeknight dinner or a special occasion. The combination of the sweet maple syrup and the tangy Dijon mustard adds depth of flavor to the salmon. Enjoy!

Vegetarian Wellington

Ingredients:

For the Filling:

- 2 tablespoons olive oil
- 1 onion, finely chopped
- 2 cloves garlic, minced
- 8 ounces (225g) mushrooms, finely chopped
- 1 cup cooked lentils
- 1 cup cooked quinoa or rice
- 1 cup fresh spinach, chopped
- 1/2 cup breadcrumbs
- 1/4 cup chopped fresh herbs (such as parsley, thyme, and rosemary)
- Salt and black pepper, to taste
- 1/2 cup grated vegetarian Parmesan or other cheese (optional)
- 1 egg, beaten (for egg wash)

For the Wellington:

- 1 sheet puff pastry, thawed if frozen
- Dijon mustard (optional, for spreading on pastry)

Instructions:

Prepare the Filling:
- In a large skillet, heat olive oil over medium heat. Add the chopped onion and cook until softened.
- Add the minced garlic and chopped mushrooms to the skillet. Cook until the mushrooms release their moisture and become golden brown.
- Stir in the cooked lentils, quinoa or rice, chopped spinach, breadcrumbs, and fresh herbs. Cook for a few more minutes until the mixture is well combined and the spinach is wilted.
- Season the filling with salt and black pepper. If using, mix in the grated vegetarian Parmesan.
- Allow the filling to cool.

Assemble the Wellington:
- Preheat your oven to 375°F (190°C).
- Roll out the puff pastry sheet on a lightly floured surface.
- Optionally, spread a thin layer of Dijon mustard on the pastry sheet, leaving a border around the edges.
- Spoon the cooled vegetable filling along the center of the pastry sheet, shaping it into a log.

Wrap the Wellington:
- Fold the sides of the puff pastry over the filling, sealing the edges. Pinch the ends to secure the filling completely.
- Place the Wellington seam side down on a baking sheet lined with parchment paper.

Brush with Egg Wash:
- Brush the surface of the Wellington with the beaten egg. This will give it a golden finish when baked.

Bake:
- Bake in the preheated oven for approximately 25-30 minutes or until the puff pastry is golden brown and crisp.

Serve:
- Allow the Vegetarian Wellington to rest for a few minutes before slicing. Serve it with your favorite vegetarian gravy or sauce.

This Vegetarian Wellington is a flavorful and satisfying dish that's sure to impress. It's a perfect centerpiece for holiday dinners or any special occasion. Customize the filling with your favorite vegetables and herbs for added variety.

Stuffed Acorn Squash with White Rice and Cranberries

Ingredients:

- 2 acorn squash, halved and seeds removed
- 1 cup white rice, cooked according to package instructions
- 1/2 cup dried cranberries
- 1/2 cup pecans, chopped
- 1/4 cup fresh parsley, chopped
- 1/4 cup feta cheese, crumbled (optional)
- 2 tablespoons olive oil
- 1 tablespoon maple syrup
- Salt and black pepper, to taste
- Ground cinnamon, for sprinkling

Instructions:

Preheat the Oven:
- Preheat your oven to 400°F (200°C).

Prepare the Acorn Squash:
- Cut the acorn squash in half and scoop out the seeds. Place the squash halves on a baking sheet, cut side up.

Season and Roast:
- Drizzle the squash halves with olive oil and maple syrup. Sprinkle with salt, black pepper, and a pinch of ground cinnamon.
- Roast in the preheated oven for 30-40 minutes or until the squash is tender.

Prepare the Filling:
- In a bowl, combine the cooked white rice, dried cranberries, chopped pecans, fresh parsley, and crumbled feta cheese (if using). Mix well.

Stuff the Squash:
- Once the acorn squash halves are done roasting, fill each half with the rice mixture, packing it down slightly.

Bake Again:
- Return the stuffed acorn squash to the oven and bake for an additional 10-15 minutes or until the filling is heated through.

Serve:
- Remove the stuffed acorn squash from the oven and let it cool for a few minutes.

- Serve each half on a plate, drizzling with any remaining maple syrup and sprinkling with additional fresh parsley if desired.

This Stuffed Acorn Squash with White Rice and Cranberries is a delicious and visually appealing dish. The combination of the sweet and nutty flavors from the squash, the tartness of the cranberries, and the crunch of pecans creates a delightful autumn-inspired meal.

Beef Wellington

Ingredients:

- 2 to 2.5 pounds (1 to 1.2 kg) beef tenderloin
- Salt and black pepper, to taste
- 2 tablespoons olive oil
- 1/2 cup Dijon mustard
- 8 slices prosciutto
- 1 pound (450g) mushrooms, finely chopped
- 2 cloves garlic, minced
- 1 tablespoon fresh thyme, chopped
- 1 tablespoon fresh parsley, chopped
- 2 tablespoons unsalted butter
- Puff pastry sheets (enough to wrap the beef)
- 1 egg, beaten (for egg wash)

Instructions:

Preheat the Oven:
- Preheat your oven to 425°F (220°C).

Prepare the Beef:
- Season the beef tenderloin with salt and black pepper.
- Heat olive oil in a skillet over high heat. Sear the beef on all sides until browned. Remove from heat and let it cool. Brush the beef with Dijon mustard.

Wrap with Prosciutto:
- Lay out a sheet of plastic wrap and arrange the prosciutto slices slightly overlapping. Place the beef on the prosciutto and roll it up tightly using the plastic wrap. Chill in the refrigerator.

Prepare the Mushroom Duxelles:
- In the same skillet, add butter and sauté chopped mushrooms, garlic, thyme, and parsley over medium heat until the mushrooms release their moisture and become golden brown. Remove excess liquid.
- Allow the mushroom mixture to cool.

Roll Out Puff Pastry:
- Roll out the puff pastry on a floured surface to a size large enough to wrap the beef completely.

Assemble the Wellington:
- Unwrap the beef from the prosciutto and place it in the center of the puff pastry.
- Spread the mushroom duxelles over the prosciutto-wrapped beef.
- Fold the puff pastry over the beef, sealing the edges. Trim any excess pastry.

Brush with Egg Wash:
- Brush the top of the puff pastry with beaten egg for a golden finish.

Bake:
- Place the Beef Wellington on a baking sheet and bake in the preheated oven for about 25-30 minutes or until the pastry is golden brown and the beef reaches your desired doneness.

Rest and Serve:
- Allow the Beef Wellington to rest for 10 minutes before slicing. Serve with your favorite sauce.

Beef Wellington is a show-stopping dish, perfect for special occasions. The combination of the tender beef, savory mushroom duxelles, and flaky puff pastry creates a delightful and impressive meal.

Herb-Roasted Chicken with Citrus Glaze

Ingredients:

For the Herb-Roasted Chicken:

- 1 whole chicken (about 4-5 pounds)
- 2 tablespoons olive oil
- 2 teaspoons dried thyme
- 2 teaspoons dried rosemary
- 2 teaspoons dried sage
- 1 teaspoon dried oregano
- Salt and black pepper, to taste
- 1 lemon, sliced

For the Citrus Glaze:

- 1/2 cup orange juice
- 1/4 cup lemon juice
- 1/4 cup honey
- 2 tablespoons Dijon mustard
- 2 cloves garlic, minced
- Salt and black pepper, to taste

Instructions:

Preheat the Oven:
- Preheat your oven to 375°F (190°C).

Prepare the Chicken:
- Pat the chicken dry with paper towels. Place it on a roasting pan or baking dish.

Herb-Roasted Chicken:
- In a small bowl, mix together the olive oil, dried thyme, dried rosemary, dried sage, dried oregano, salt, and black pepper to create an herb rub.
- Rub the herb mixture all over the chicken, including under the skin if possible.
- Place lemon slices under the skin and inside the cavity of the chicken.

Roast the Chicken:
- Roast the chicken in the preheated oven for about 1 to 1.5 hours or until the internal temperature reaches 165°F (74°C) and the skin is golden brown.

Prepare the Citrus Glaze:
- In a small saucepan, combine orange juice, lemon juice, honey, Dijon mustard, minced garlic, salt, and black pepper.
- Bring the mixture to a simmer over medium heat, stirring occasionally. Cook for about 5-7 minutes or until the glaze thickens slightly.

Glaze the Chicken:
- During the last 20-30 minutes of roasting, brush the chicken with the citrus glaze every 10 minutes to create a glossy finish.

Rest and Serve:
- Once the chicken is cooked, let it rest for about 10-15 minutes before carving.
- Serve the herb-roasted chicken with additional citrus glaze on the side.

This Herb-Roasted Chicken with Citrus Glaze is a delightful blend of savory and tangy flavors, making it a perfect choice for a special dinner. The combination of herbs and citrus not only adds depth to the chicken but also provides a beautiful aroma while roasting.

Pomegranate Glazed Pork Tenderloin

Ingredients:

- 2 pork tenderloins (about 1.5 to 2 pounds total)
- Salt and black pepper, to taste
- 2 tablespoons olive oil
- 1 teaspoon ground cumin
- 1 teaspoon ground coriander
- 1/2 teaspoon ground cinnamon
- 1/2 teaspoon smoked paprika
- 1 cup pomegranate juice
- 1/4 cup honey
- 2 tablespoons balsamic vinegar
- 2 cloves garlic, minced
- Pomegranate arils (seeds) for garnish (optional)
- Fresh parsley, chopped, for garnish (optional)

Instructions:

Preheat the Oven:
- Preheat your oven to 400°F (200°C).

Prepare the Pork Tenderloins:
- Pat the pork tenderloins dry with paper towels. Season them with salt and black pepper.

Sear the Pork:
- In an ovenproof skillet, heat olive oil over medium-high heat. Sear the pork tenderloins on all sides until browned.

Prepare the Spice Rub:
- In a small bowl, mix together ground cumin, ground coriander, ground cinnamon, smoked paprika, and a pinch of salt.

Rub the Pork with Spices:
- Rub the spice mixture over the seared pork tenderloins.

Roast in the Oven:
- Transfer the skillet to the preheated oven and roast for about 15-20 minutes or until the internal temperature reaches 145°F (63°C) for medium doneness.

Prepare the Pomegranate Glaze:

- While the pork is roasting, prepare the pomegranate glaze. In a saucepan, combine pomegranate juice, honey, balsamic vinegar, and minced garlic. Bring to a simmer over medium heat and cook for about 10-12 minutes or until the glaze thickens.

Glaze the Pork:
- Brush the roasted pork tenderloins with the pomegranate glaze during the last 5 minutes of cooking and continue to roast until the glaze is caramelized.

Rest and Serve:
- Remove the pork from the oven and let it rest for a few minutes before slicing. Brush with any remaining glaze.
- Garnish with pomegranate arils and chopped fresh parsley if desired.

This Pomegranate Glazed Pork Tenderloin is a delightful combination of sweet and savory flavors, making it a perfect option for a special dinner or festive occasion. The pomegranate glaze adds a beautiful shine and a burst of fruity goodness to the tender pork.

Vegetarian Stuffed Bell Peppers

Ingredients:

- 4 large bell peppers (any color), halved and seeds removed
- 1 cup quinoa or rice, cooked according to package instructions
- 1 tablespoon olive oil
- 1 onion, finely chopped
- 2 cloves garlic, minced
- 1 zucchini, diced
- 1 carrot, grated
- 1 cup cherry tomatoes, halved
- 1 cup black beans, drained and rinsed
- 1 cup corn kernels (fresh, frozen, or canned)
- 1 teaspoon ground cumin
- 1 teaspoon chili powder
- Salt and black pepper, to taste
- 1 cup shredded cheese (cheddar, Monterey Jack, or your choice)
- Fresh cilantro or parsley, chopped, for garnish
- Salsa or guacamole, for serving (optional)

Instructions:

Preheat the Oven:
- Preheat your oven to 375°F (190°C).

Prepare the Bell Peppers:
- Cut the bell peppers in half lengthwise, removing the seeds and membranes. Place the pepper halves in a baking dish.

Prepare the Filling:
- In a large skillet, heat olive oil over medium heat. Add chopped onion and garlic, sautéing until softened.
- Add diced zucchini and grated carrot to the skillet. Cook for a few minutes until the vegetables are tender.
- Stir in cherry tomatoes, black beans, and corn. Season with ground cumin, chili powder, salt, and black pepper. Cook for an additional 2-3 minutes.
- In a large bowl, combine the cooked quinoa or rice with the vegetable mixture. Mix well.

Fill the Bell Peppers:

- Stuff each bell pepper half with the quinoa and vegetable mixture, pressing it down gently.

Bake:
- Cover the baking dish with foil and bake in the preheated oven for 25-30 minutes or until the peppers are tender.

Add Cheese and Bake Again:
- Remove the foil and sprinkle shredded cheese over the stuffed peppers. Return to the oven and bake for an additional 5-7 minutes or until the cheese is melted and bubbly.

Garnish and Serve:
- Remove the stuffed peppers from the oven and let them cool slightly. Garnish with chopped cilantro or parsley.
- Serve the vegetarian stuffed bell peppers with salsa or guacamole on the side, if desired.

These Vegetarian Stuffed Bell Peppers are not only nutritious but also visually appealing, making them a great option for a meatless dinner. Feel free to customize the filling with your favorite vegetables and spices.

Sides:

Garlic Mashed Potatoes

Ingredients:

- 2 pounds (about 1 kg) potatoes (russet or Yukon Gold), peeled and cut into chunks
- 4 cloves garlic, minced
- 1/2 cup unsalted butter
- 1 cup milk or cream
- Salt and black pepper, to taste
- Fresh chives or parsley, chopped (for garnish, optional)

Instructions:

Boil the Potatoes:
- Place the potato chunks in a large pot and cover with cold water. Add a pinch of salt.
- Bring the water to a boil and cook the potatoes until fork-tender, usually about 15-20 minutes.

Prepare the Garlic:
- In a small saucepan, melt the butter over low heat. Add the minced garlic and cook for 1-2 minutes until fragrant. Be careful not to let the garlic brown.

Drain and Mash:
- Drain the potatoes and return them to the pot.
- Mash the potatoes using a potato masher or a hand mixer until smooth and lump-free.

Add Garlic Butter:
- Pour the melted garlic butter over the mashed potatoes.

Add Milk or Cream:
- Gradually add the milk or cream to the potatoes, mixing continuously, until you achieve your desired creamy consistency. Adjust the amount of milk or cream to your liking.

Season:
- Season the mashed potatoes with salt and black pepper. Taste and adjust the seasoning as needed.

Garnish and Serve:

- Transfer the garlic mashed potatoes to a serving bowl.
- Garnish with chopped fresh chives or parsley if desired.

Garlic mashed potatoes are a versatile side dish that complements roasted meats, grilled chicken, or vegetarian dishes. They add a rich and savory element to your meal. Adjust the garlic and butter to suit your taste preferences, and enjoy this classic comfort food.

Roasted Brussel Sprouts with Balsamic Glaze

Ingredients:

- 1 pound Brussels sprouts, trimmed and halved
- 2 tablespoons olive oil
- Salt and black pepper, to taste
- 2 tablespoons balsamic glaze (store-bought or homemade)
- 2 tablespoons grated Parmesan cheese (optional)
- Chopped fresh parsley for garnish (optional)

Instructions:

Preheat the Oven:
- Preheat your oven to 400°F (200°C).

Prepare the Brussels Sprouts:
- Trim the ends of the Brussels sprouts and cut them in half.

Toss with Olive Oil:
- In a bowl, toss the halved Brussels sprouts with olive oil until they are well coated.

Season:
- Season the Brussels sprouts with salt and black pepper to taste. Toss again to ensure even seasoning.

Roast in the Oven:
- Spread the Brussels sprouts in a single layer on a baking sheet lined with parchment paper.
- Roast in the preheated oven for 20-25 minutes or until the Brussels sprouts are golden brown and crispy on the edges. Stir or shake the pan halfway through for even roasting.

Finish with Balsamic Glaze:
- Drizzle the roasted Brussels sprouts with balsamic glaze while they are still hot. Toss gently to coat.

Optional Parmesan Cheese:
- If desired, sprinkle grated Parmesan cheese over the Brussels sprouts and toss lightly.

Garnish and Serve:
- Transfer the roasted Brussels sprouts to a serving dish. Garnish with chopped fresh parsley if desired.

Roasted Brussels Sprouts with Balsamic Glaze make a delicious and elegant side dish that's perfect for holiday dinners or any meal. The balsamic glaze adds a sweet and tangy flavor that complements the caramelized Brussels sprouts, creating a dish that's both savory and slightly sweet.

Cranberry Orange Quinoa Salad

Ingredients:

For the Salad:

- 1 cup quinoa, rinsed
- 2 cups water
- 1 cup fresh cranberries
- 1 orange, peeled and segmented
- 1/2 cup chopped pecans or walnuts, toasted
- 1/4 cup red onion, finely chopped
- 1/4 cup fresh parsley, chopped

For the Dressing:

- 3 tablespoons olive oil
- 2 tablespoons orange juice
- 1 tablespoon balsamic vinegar
- 1 tablespoon honey or maple syrup
- Salt and black pepper, to taste

Instructions:

Cook the Quinoa:
- In a medium saucepan, combine quinoa and water. Bring to a boil, then reduce the heat to low, cover, and simmer for 15-20 minutes, or until the quinoa is cooked and the water is absorbed. Fluff the quinoa with a fork and let it cool.

Prepare the Cranberries:
- If using fresh cranberries, pulse them in a food processor until coarsely chopped. If using dried cranberries, no additional preparation is needed.

Toast the Nuts:
- In a dry skillet over medium heat, toast the chopped pecans or walnuts until they become fragrant. Be careful not to burn them. Set aside to cool.

Assemble the Salad:

- In a large bowl, combine the cooked quinoa, chopped cranberries, orange segments, toasted nuts, chopped red onion, and fresh parsley.

Make the Dressing:
- In a small bowl, whisk together the olive oil, orange juice, balsamic vinegar, honey or maple syrup, salt, and black pepper.

Dress the Salad:
- Pour the dressing over the salad and toss until all ingredients are well coated.

Chill and Serve:
- Refrigerate the salad for at least 30 minutes before serving to allow the flavors to meld.

Garnish and Enjoy:
- Before serving, garnish the salad with additional fresh parsley if desired. Serve chilled.

This Cranberry Orange Quinoa Salad is a light and nutritious option that works well as a side dish or a standalone meal. The combination of quinoa, cranberries, orange, and nuts creates a delightful balance of flavors and textures. Enjoy!

Creamy Green Bean Casserole

Ingredients:

- 1 1/2 pounds fresh green beans, trimmed and cut into bite-sized pieces
- 2 tablespoons unsalted butter
- 1 pound cremini or button mushrooms, sliced
- 3 cloves garlic, minced
- 1/4 cup all-purpose flour
- 1 1/2 cups chicken or vegetable broth
- 1 1/2 cups whole milk
- Salt and black pepper, to taste
- 1 teaspoon soy sauce
- 1/2 teaspoon dried thyme
- 1/2 cup grated Parmesan cheese
- 2 cans (6 ounces each) crispy fried onions (French's or homemade)

Instructions:

Preheat the Oven:
- Preheat your oven to 375°F (190°C).

Blanch the Green Beans:
- Bring a large pot of salted water to a boil. Add the green beans and cook for 3-4 minutes until they are bright green and slightly tender. Drain and immediately transfer to an ice water bath to stop the cooking process. Drain again and set aside.

Prepare the Mushroom Sauce:
- In a large skillet, melt the butter over medium heat. Add sliced mushrooms and sauté until they release their moisture and become golden brown.
- Add minced garlic and cook for an additional 1-2 minutes.
- Sprinkle the flour over the mushrooms and stir to coat them evenly. Cook for 1-2 minutes to eliminate the raw flour taste.
- Gradually whisk in the chicken or vegetable broth and then the milk, stirring constantly to avoid lumps.
- Season the sauce with salt, black pepper, soy sauce, and dried thyme. Simmer for 5-7 minutes, or until the sauce thickens.

Combine Green Beans and Sauce:

- Add the blanched green beans to the mushroom sauce, stirring until the beans are well coated.
- Stir in the grated Parmesan cheese until it is melted and incorporated into the sauce.

Transfer to Casserole Dish:
- Transfer the green bean mixture to a greased 9x13-inch baking dish or a similar-sized casserole dish.

Top with Fried Onions:
- Sprinkle the crispy fried onions evenly over the top of the green bean mixture.

Bake:
- Bake in the preheated oven for 25-30 minutes or until the casserole is hot and bubbly, and the fried onions are golden brown.

Serve:
- Remove from the oven and let it rest for a few minutes before serving.

This Creamy Green Bean Casserole is a crowd-pleaser, and it's a great addition to holiday feasts or any special occasion. The combination of the creamy mushroom sauce and the crispy fried onions creates a comforting and satisfying dish.

Sweet Potato Casserole with Pecan Streusel

Ingredients:

For the Sweet Potato Filling:

- 4 cups mashed sweet potatoes (about 3-4 large sweet potatoes, cooked and peeled)
- 1/2 cup unsalted butter, melted
- 1/2 cup milk (whole or evaporated)
- 1/2 cup granulated sugar
- 2 large eggs, beaten
- 1 teaspoon vanilla extract
- 1/2 teaspoon salt

For the Pecan Streusel Topping:

- 1 cup chopped pecans
- 1/2 cup all-purpose flour
- 1/2 cup brown sugar, packed
- 1/4 cup unsalted butter, melted
- 1/2 teaspoon ground cinnamon
- Pinch of salt

Instructions:

Preheat the Oven:
- Preheat your oven to 350°F (175°C).

Prepare the Sweet Potatoes:
- Cook the sweet potatoes until tender. Mash them in a large mixing bowl.

Make the Sweet Potato Filling:
- To the mashed sweet potatoes, add melted butter, milk, granulated sugar, beaten eggs, vanilla extract, and salt. Mix until well combined and smooth.

Transfer to Casserole Dish:
- Transfer the sweet potato mixture to a greased 9x13-inch baking dish or a similar-sized casserole dish.

Prepare the Pecan Streusel Topping:
- In a separate bowl, combine chopped pecans, all-purpose flour, brown sugar, melted butter, ground cinnamon, and a pinch of salt. Mix until the streusel is crumbly.

Top the Sweet Potatoes:
- Sprinkle the pecan streusel topping evenly over the sweet potato mixture in the casserole dish.

Bake:
- Bake in the preheated oven for 25-30 minutes or until the sweet potato filling is set and the streusel is golden brown.

Serve:
- Remove from the oven and let it cool slightly before serving.

Optional Additions:

- For an extra layer of sweetness, you can add miniature marshmallows on top during the last 5-10 minutes of baking until they are golden and gooey.

This Sweet Potato Casserole with Pecan Streusel is a comforting and flavorful side dish that's perfect for holiday gatherings or any special occasion. The combination of creamy sweet potatoes and the crunchy, nutty streusel topping creates a delightful contrast in texture and taste.

Butternut Squash and Sage Risotto

Ingredients:

- 1 small butternut squash, peeled, seeded, and diced into small cubes
- 2 tablespoons olive oil
- Salt and black pepper, to taste
- 1 cup Arborio rice
- 1/2 cup dry white wine (optional)
- 1 small onion, finely chopped
- 2 cloves garlic, minced
- 6-8 fresh sage leaves, chopped
- 4 cups vegetable or chicken broth, kept warm
- 1/2 cup Parmesan cheese, grated
- 2 tablespoons unsalted butter
- Additional sage leaves for garnish (optional)

Instructions:

Roast the Butternut Squash:
- Preheat your oven to 400°F (200°C).
- Toss the diced butternut squash with 1 tablespoon of olive oil, salt, and black pepper. Spread it on a baking sheet in a single layer.
- Roast in the preheated oven for 20-25 minutes or until the squash is tender and slightly caramelized. Set aside.

Prepare the Risotto Base:
- In a large skillet or wide saucepan, heat the remaining 1 tablespoon of olive oil over medium heat.
- Add chopped onion and cook until it becomes translucent, about 2-3 minutes.
- Stir in minced garlic and chopped sage leaves. Cook for an additional 1-2 minutes until fragrant.
- Add Arborio rice to the pan and cook, stirring frequently, until the rice is lightly toasted.

Deglaze with Wine (Optional):
- Pour in the white wine and stir until most of it has evaporated.

Add Broth Gradually:
- Begin adding warm broth to the rice mixture one ladleful at a time. Allow the liquid to be absorbed before adding the next ladleful.

- Continue this process, stirring frequently, until the rice is creamy and al dente. This will take about 18-20 minutes.

Incorporate Roasted Butternut Squash:
- Fold in the roasted butternut squash cubes during the last 5 minutes of cooking. This allows them to blend into the risotto while maintaining their shape.

Finish with Butter and Parmesan:
- Stir in the grated Parmesan cheese and unsalted butter, creating a creamy and velvety texture.

Adjust Seasoning:
- Season the risotto with salt and black pepper to taste. Adjust the consistency with additional warm broth if needed.

Serve and Garnish:
- Serve the Butternut Squash and Sage Risotto in bowls, garnishing with additional sage leaves if desired.

This Butternut Squash and Sage Risotto is a comforting and flavorful dish that captures the essence of fall. The creamy texture of the risotto combined with the sweetness of the roasted butternut squash and the earthy aroma of sage creates a delightful culinary experience.

Cranberry Walnut Stuffing

Ingredients:

- 8 cups day-old bread, cut into cubes (white, whole wheat, or a mix)
- 1/2 cup unsalted butter
- 1 large onion, finely chopped
- 2 celery stalks, finely chopped
- 2 cloves garlic, minced
- 1 cup dried cranberries
- 1 cup chopped walnuts, toasted
- 2 teaspoons dried sage
- 1 teaspoon dried thyme
- 1 teaspoon dried rosemary
- Salt and black pepper, to taste
- 2 to 3 cups chicken or vegetable broth (as needed for moistening)
- Fresh parsley, chopped, for garnish (optional)

Instructions:

Preheat the Oven:
- Preheat your oven to 350°F (175°C).

Prepare the Bread Cubes:
- Spread the bread cubes on a baking sheet and toast them in the preheated oven for about 10-15 minutes or until they are lightly browned and crisp. Allow them to cool.

Sauté Vegetables:
- In a large skillet, melt the butter over medium heat. Add the chopped onion and celery, sautéing until softened, about 5-7 minutes.
- Add minced garlic to the skillet and cook for an additional 1-2 minutes until fragrant.

Combine Ingredients:
- In a large mixing bowl, combine the toasted bread cubes, sautéed vegetables, dried cranberries, toasted walnuts, dried sage, dried thyme, dried rosemary, salt, and black pepper. Toss everything together until well mixed.

Moisten with Broth:
- Gradually pour the chicken or vegetable broth over the bread mixture, stirring well after each addition. Add enough broth to achieve your desired

level of moistness. The bread should be evenly moistened but not overly wet.

Bake:
- Transfer the stuffing mixture to a greased baking dish. Cover with aluminum foil.
- Bake in the preheated oven for 30 minutes. Then, remove the foil and bake for an additional 15-20 minutes or until the top is golden brown and crisp.

Garnish and Serve:
- Remove from the oven and let the stuffing rest for a few minutes before serving. Garnish with chopped fresh parsley if desired.

This Cranberry Walnut Stuffing is a delightful side dish that complements roasted turkey, chicken, or pork. The combination of sweet cranberries, crunchy walnuts, and aromatic herbs makes it a flavorful addition to your holiday table.

Maple Glazed Carrots

Ingredients:

- 1 pound (about 450g) carrots, peeled and sliced into thin rounds or matchsticks
- 2 tablespoons unsalted butter
- 2 tablespoons pure maple syrup
- 1 tablespoon brown sugar
- 1/2 teaspoon ground cinnamon
- Salt and black pepper, to taste
- Fresh parsley, chopped, for garnish (optional)

Instructions:

Prepare the Carrots:
- Peel and slice the carrots into thin rounds or matchsticks, ensuring they are of uniform size for even cooking.

Cook the Carrots:
- In a large skillet, melt the butter over medium heat. Add the sliced carrots and sauté for 3-5 minutes until they start to soften.

Add Maple Glaze:
- Drizzle the pure maple syrup over the carrots and sprinkle brown sugar and ground cinnamon. Toss the carrots to coat them evenly with the glaze.

Simmer:
- Reduce the heat to low, cover the skillet, and let the carrots simmer for an additional 10-15 minutes or until they are tender. Stir occasionally to prevent sticking.

Season:
- Season the glazed carrots with salt and black pepper to taste. Adjust the sweetness or spiciness according to your preference.

Garnish and Serve:
- Transfer the maple glazed carrots to a serving dish. Garnish with chopped fresh parsley if desired.

Serve Warm:
- Serve the maple glazed carrots warm as a side dish for holiday dinners, Sunday roasts, or any special occasion.

These Maple Glazed Carrots are a delightful balance of sweetness and warmth. The natural sweetness of maple syrup enhances the flavor of the carrots, while a hint of cinnamon adds a touch of spice. This simple yet elegant side dish is sure to be a hit on your table.

Creamed Corn Casserole

Ingredients:

- 4 cups frozen or canned corn kernels (drained if using canned)
- 1/2 cup unsalted butter, melted
- 1 cup sour cream
- 1 cup shredded cheddar cheese
- 1/2 cup grated Parmesan cheese
- 1 cup cornbread mix
- 2 large eggs, beaten
- 1/4 cup chopped fresh parsley (optional, for garnish)
- Salt and black pepper, to taste

Instructions:

Preheat the Oven:
- Preheat your oven to 350°F (175°C). Grease a 9x13-inch baking dish.

Combine Ingredients:
- In a large mixing bowl, combine the corn kernels, melted butter, sour cream, shredded cheddar cheese, Parmesan cheese, cornbread mix, beaten eggs, salt, and black pepper. Mix until well combined.

Transfer to Baking Dish:
- Transfer the corn mixture to the greased baking dish, spreading it evenly.

Bake:
- Bake in the preheated oven for 45-50 minutes or until the top is golden brown and the casserole is set.

Garnish and Serve:
- Remove from the oven and let it cool for a few minutes. Garnish with chopped fresh parsley if desired.

Serve Warm:
- Serve the Creamed Corn Casserole warm as a side dish alongside your favorite main courses.

This Creamed Corn Casserole is a comforting and slightly sweet dish that pairs well with roasted meats, grilled chicken, or as part of a holiday feast. The combination of creamy texture and cornbread flavor makes it a crowd-pleaser.

Hasselback Potatoes with Rosemary and Garlic

Ingredients:

- 4 large russet potatoes
- 4 tablespoons unsalted butter, melted
- 4 cloves garlic, thinly sliced
- 2 tablespoons fresh rosemary, chopped
- Salt and black pepper, to taste
- Olive oil (for drizzling)
- Grated Parmesan cheese (optional, for garnish)
- Chopped fresh parsley (optional, for garnish)

Instructions:

Preheat the Oven:
- Preheat your oven to 425°F (220°C).

Prepare the Potatoes:
- Scrub the potatoes clean, and pat them dry. Place a potato between the handles of two wooden spoons or chopsticks (this prevents you from cutting all the way through).

Make Hasselback Cuts:
- Make thin slices across the potato, cutting about 80% of the way through, leaving the bottom intact. The wooden spoons or chopsticks will prevent you from accidentally cutting all the way through.

Prepare Garlic and Rosemary Mixture:
- In a small bowl, mix melted butter, sliced garlic, and chopped rosemary. Season with salt and black pepper to taste.

Coat Potatoes:
- Place the sliced potatoes on a baking sheet. Brush the butter, garlic, and rosemary mixture over each potato, making sure to get the flavors between the slices.

Drizzle with Olive Oil:
- Drizzle the potatoes with a bit of olive oil for extra crispiness.

Bake:
- Bake in the preheated oven for about 45-55 minutes or until the potatoes are crispy on the edges and tender on the inside. If the tops start to brown too quickly, cover with foil and continue baking.

Optional Garnishes:

- Optionally, sprinkle grated Parmesan cheese and chopped fresh parsley over the potatoes during the last 10 minutes of baking.

Serve Warm:
- Remove from the oven and let the Hasselback Potatoes rest for a few minutes before serving.

These Hasselback Potatoes with Rosemary and Garlic make an elegant and delicious side dish that's perfect for special occasions or any meal. The accordion-like cuts create a crispy texture, while the garlic and rosemary infuse the potatoes with incredible flavor.

Desserts:

Classic Christmas Cookies (Sugar, Gingerbread, Peppermint)

Classic Sugar Cookies:

Ingredients:

- 2 3/4 cups all-purpose flour
- 1 teaspoon baking soda
- 1/2 teaspoon baking powder
- 1 cup unsalted butter, softened
- 1 1/2 cups granulated sugar
- 1 large egg
- 1 teaspoon vanilla extract
- 1/2 teaspoon almond extract (optional)
- Additional sugar for rolling (optional)

Instructions:

Preheat the Oven:
- Preheat your oven to 375°F (190°C). Line baking sheets with parchment paper.

Combine Dry Ingredients:
- In a medium bowl, whisk together the flour, baking soda, and baking powder. Set aside.

Cream Butter and Sugar:
- In a large mixing bowl, cream together the softened butter and sugar until light and fluffy.

Add Wet Ingredients:
- Beat in the egg, vanilla extract, and almond extract (if using) until well combined.

Gradually Add Dry Ingredients:
- Gradually add the dry ingredients to the wet ingredients, mixing until just combined.

Shape and Bake:
- Shape the dough into 1-inch balls and roll them in additional sugar if desired. Place them on the prepared baking sheets.
- Bake for 8-10 minutes or until the edges are lightly golden. Allow the cookies to cool on the baking sheets for a few minutes before transferring them to a wire rack to cool completely.

Classic Gingerbread Cookies:

Ingredients:

- 3 cups all-purpose flour
- 1 1/2 teaspoons ground ginger
- 1 1/2 teaspoons ground cinnamon
- 1/2 teaspoon ground cloves
- 1/2 teaspoon baking soda
- 1/4 teaspoon salt
- 3/4 cup unsalted butter, softened
- 3/4 cup brown sugar, packed
- 1/2 cup molasses
- 1 large egg

Instructions:

Preheat the Oven:
- Preheat your oven to 350°F (175°C). Line baking sheets with parchment paper.

Combine Dry Ingredients:
- In a medium bowl, whisk together the flour, ginger, cinnamon, cloves, baking soda, and salt. Set aside.

Cream Butter and Sugar:
- In a large mixing bowl, cream together the softened butter and brown sugar until light and fluffy.

Add Molasses and Egg:
- Beat in the molasses and egg until well combined.

Gradually Add Dry Ingredients:
- Gradually add the dry ingredients to the wet ingredients, mixing until just combined.

Chill and Roll:
- Divide the dough into two portions, wrap each in plastic wrap, and chill for at least 2 hours.
- Roll out the chilled dough on a floured surface to about 1/4-inch thickness. Cut out gingerbread shapes with cookie cutters.

Bake:
- Place the cut-out cookies on the prepared baking sheets and bake for 8-10 minutes or until the edges are set. Allow the cookies to cool on the baking sheets for a few minutes before transferring them to a wire rack to cool completely.

Classic Peppermint Cookies:

Ingredients:

- 2 1/2 cups all-purpose flour
- 1/2 teaspoon baking powder
- 1/4 teaspoon salt
- 1 cup unsalted butter, softened
- 1 cup granulated sugar
- 1 large egg
- 1 teaspoon peppermint extract
- Crushed candy canes for rolling

Instructions:

Preheat the Oven:
- Preheat your oven to 350°F (175°C). Line baking sheets with parchment paper.

Combine Dry Ingredients:
- In a medium bowl, whisk together the flour, baking powder, and salt. Set aside.

Cream Butter and Sugar:
- In a large mixing bowl, cream together the softened butter and granulated sugar until light and fluffy.

Add Egg and Peppermint Extract:
- Beat in the egg and peppermint extract until well combined.

Gradually Add Dry Ingredients:
- Gradually add the dry ingredients to the wet ingredients, mixing until just combined.

Chill and Roll:
- Divide the dough into two portions, wrap each in plastic wrap, and chill for at least 1 hour.
- Roll tablespoon-sized portions of dough into balls and roll them in crushed candy canes.

Bake:
- Place the coated cookies on the prepared baking sheets and bake for 10-12 minutes or until the edges are set. Allow the cookies to cool on the baking sheets for a few minutes before transferring them to a wire rack to cool completely.

These classic Christmas cookies will add a festive touch to your holiday celebrations! Enjoy baking and sharing these delicious treats.

Yule Log Cake (Bûche de Noël)

Ingredients:

For the Cake:

- 4 large eggs, separated
- 3/4 cup granulated sugar
- 1 teaspoon vanilla extract
- 1/4 cup cocoa powder
- 1/4 cup all-purpose flour
- 1/4 teaspoon salt

For the Filling:

- 1 1/2 cups heavy cream
- 1/4 cup powdered sugar
- 1 teaspoon vanilla extract

For the Ganache:

- 8 ounces semisweet or bittersweet chocolate, finely chopped
- 1 cup heavy cream
- 2 tablespoons unsalted butter

Instructions:

Cake:

Preheat the Oven:
- Preheat your oven to 350°F (175°C). Grease and line a 10x15-inch jelly roll pan with parchment paper.

Prepare the Batter:
- In a large bowl, beat egg yolks and sugar until thick and pale. Stir in the vanilla extract.
- In a separate bowl, sift together cocoa powder, flour, and salt. Gradually add the dry ingredients to the egg yolk mixture and mix until well combined.

Whip Egg Whites:

- In another clean, dry bowl, whip the egg whites until stiff peaks form. Gently fold the whipped egg whites into the chocolate batter until no white streaks remain.

Bake:
- Spread the batter evenly in the prepared jelly roll pan. Bake for about 12-15 minutes or until the cake springs back when lightly touched.

Roll the Cake:
- While the cake is still warm, turn it out onto a clean kitchen towel dusted with powdered sugar. Roll the cake and towel together from the short end. Allow it to cool completely.

Filling:

Whip the Cream:
- In a bowl, whip the heavy cream, powdered sugar, and vanilla extract until stiff peaks form.

Unroll the Cake:
- Carefully unroll the cooled cake. Spread the whipped cream evenly over the cake.

Roll the Cake Again:
- Roll the cake back up, this time without the towel. Place the seam side down on a serving platter.

Ganache:

Make the Ganache:
- In a heatproof bowl, place the finely chopped chocolate. In a saucepan, heat the heavy cream until it just begins to boil. Pour the hot cream over the chocolate and let it sit for a minute. Stir until smooth. Add the butter and stir until melted.

Cover the Cake:
- Pour the ganache over the rolled cake, spreading it with a spatula to cover the entire surface.

Create Bark Texture (Optional):
- Use a fork to create a bark-like texture on the ganache.

Chill:
- Refrigerate the Yule Log Cake for at least 2 hours or overnight.

Decorate (Optional):

- Decorate your Yule Log Cake with powdered sugar, cocoa powder, or festive decorations like meringue mushrooms, holly leaves, or sugared cranberries.

Slice and Serve:
- Before serving, slice the Yule Log Cake into rounds to reveal the log shape.

This Chocolate Yule Log Cake is a beautiful and delicious centerpiece for your holiday celebrations. Feel free to get creative with decorations to make it uniquely festive!

Eggnog Cheesecake

Ingredients:

For the Crust:

- 1 1/2 cups graham cracker crumbs
- 1/4 cup unsalted butter, melted
- 1/4 cup granulated sugar

For the Cheesecake Filling:

- 4 packages (8 ounces each) cream cheese, softened
- 1 cup granulated sugar
- 3 tablespoons all-purpose flour
- 1 cup eggnog
- 4 large eggs
- 1 teaspoon vanilla extract
- 1/2 teaspoon ground nutmeg
- 1/4 teaspoon salt

For the Eggnog Glaze (optional):

- 1/2 cup powdered sugar
- 2 tablespoons eggnog
- Ground nutmeg for sprinkling

Instructions:

Crust:

Preheat the Oven:
- Preheat your oven to 325°F (160°C). Grease a 9-inch springform pan.

Make the Crust:

- In a medium bowl, combine graham cracker crumbs, melted butter, and sugar. Press the mixture into the bottom of the prepared springform pan to create an even crust.

Bake:
- Bake the crust in the preheated oven for 10 minutes. Remove from the oven and let it cool while you prepare the cheesecake filling.

Cheesecake Filling:

Prepare the Filling:
- In a large mixing bowl, beat the softened cream cheese until smooth.
- Add sugar and flour, and beat until well combined.
- Gradually add eggnog, mixing until smooth and creamy.
- Add eggs one at a time, beating well after each addition.
- Stir in vanilla extract, ground nutmeg, and salt until evenly incorporated.

Pour the Filling:
- Pour the cheesecake filling over the prepared crust in the springform pan.

Bake:
- Bake in the preheated oven for 55-60 minutes or until the center is set and the top is lightly golden.

Cool:
- Allow the cheesecake to cool in the pan for about 10 minutes, then run a knife around the edges to loosen it. Let it cool completely on a wire rack.

Eggnog Glaze (Optional):

Make the Glaze:
- In a small bowl, whisk together powdered sugar and eggnog until smooth.

Drizzle and Garnish:
- Drizzle the eggnog glaze over the cooled cheesecake. Sprinkle ground nutmeg on top for a festive touch.

Chill:
- Refrigerate the cheesecake for at least 4 hours or overnight before serving.

Serve:
- Slice and serve the Eggnog Cheesecake chilled. Enjoy the rich and creamy holiday flavors!

This Eggnog Cheesecake is a wonderful addition to your holiday dessert table, and it's sure to be a hit with eggnog lovers. The creamy texture and subtle nutmeg flavor make it a perfect festive treat.

Peppermint Bark

Ingredients:

- 12 ounces (340g) high-quality dark chocolate, chopped
- 12 ounces (340g) high-quality white chocolate, chopped
- 1/2 teaspoon peppermint extract
- 1 cup (about 120g) crushed candy canes or peppermint candies, divided

Instructions:

Prepare the Baking Sheet:
- Line a baking sheet with parchment paper or a silicone baking mat. Make sure it fits in your refrigerator or freezer.

Melt the Dark Chocolate:
- In a heatproof bowl set over a pot of simmering water (double boiler), melt the dark chocolate, stirring until smooth. Alternatively, you can melt the dark chocolate in the microwave in short bursts, stirring between each burst.

Add Peppermint Extract:
- Once the dark chocolate is melted, stir in 1/4 teaspoon of peppermint extract. Adjust the amount to your taste preference.

Spread Dark Chocolate:
- Pour the melted dark chocolate onto the prepared baking sheet and spread it into an even layer with a spatula.

Chill the Dark Chocolate:
- Place the baking sheet in the refrigerator or freezer to allow the dark chocolate to set. This should take about 15-20 minutes.

Melt the White Chocolate:
- In a clean bowl, melt the white chocolate using the same method as the dark chocolate.

Add Peppermint Extract and Candy Canes:
- Stir in the remaining 1/4 teaspoon of peppermint extract into the white chocolate. Then, fold in half of the crushed candy canes or peppermint candies.

Spread White Chocolate:
- Take the baking sheet with the set dark chocolate out of the refrigerator or freezer. Pour the melted white chocolate mixture over the dark chocolate layer and spread it evenly.

Sprinkle Remaining Candy Canes:
- Sprinkle the remaining crushed candy canes or peppermint candies over the white chocolate layer, pressing them down slightly with a spatula.

Chill the Peppermint Bark:
- Return the baking sheet to the refrigerator or freezer and chill until the Peppermint Bark is completely set and firm.

Break into Pieces:
- Once fully set, remove the Peppermint Bark from the refrigerator or freezer. Use your hands or a knife to break it into irregular pieces.

Serve or Package:
- Serve the Peppermint Bark as a festive treat or package it in decorative bags for holiday gifting.

Peppermint Bark is a wonderful holiday treat that combines the sweetness of chocolate with the cool, refreshing taste of peppermint. It's perfect for sharing with friends and family or as a delightful homemade gift during the festive season.

Pecan Pie Bars

Ingredients:

For the Crust:

- 1 1/2 cups all-purpose flour
- 1/2 cup unsalted butter, softened
- 1/4 cup granulated sugar
- 1/4 teaspoon salt

For the Pecan Filling:

- 3/4 cup unsalted butter
- 1 cup packed brown sugar
- 1/2 cup light corn syrup
- 1/4 cup honey
- 2 cups chopped pecans
- 1 teaspoon vanilla extract
- 1/4 teaspoon salt

Instructions:

Crust:

Preheat the Oven:
- Preheat your oven to 350°F (175°C). Grease a 9x13-inch baking pan.

Make the Crust:
- In a medium bowl, combine flour, softened butter, sugar, and salt. Mix until the ingredients come together and form a crumbly dough.
- Press the crust mixture evenly into the bottom of the prepared baking pan.

Bake the Crust:
- Bake the crust in the preheated oven for about 15-18 minutes or until it's lightly golden. Remove from the oven and set aside.

Pecan Filling:

Prepare the Filling:
- In a saucepan over medium heat, melt the butter. Add brown sugar, corn syrup, honey, chopped pecans, vanilla extract, and salt.

- Stir the mixture continuously until it comes to a gentle boil. Allow it to simmer for 2-3 minutes while stirring. Remove from heat.

Pour the Filling:
- Pour the pecan filling over the pre-baked crust, spreading it evenly.

Bake Again:
- Return the pan to the oven and bake for an additional 20-25 minutes or until the filling is set and slightly golden.

Cool and Slice:
- Allow the Pecan Pie Bars to cool completely in the pan. Once cooled, you can refrigerate them to make slicing easier.

Slice into Bars:
- Use a sharp knife to slice the cooled pecan bars into squares or rectangles.

Serve:
- Serve the Pecan Pie Bars as a delightful dessert, and optionally, dust with powdered sugar for a decorative touch.

These Pecan Pie Bars are a crowd-pleaser, offering all the flavors of a classic pecan pie in a convenient and shareable form. They make a wonderful addition to holiday dessert tables or any special occasion.

Drinks:

Spiced Mulled Wine

Ingredients:

- 1 bottle (750 ml) red wine (use a bold and fruity variety)
- 1 orange, sliced
- 1/4 cup brandy (optional)
- 1/4 cup honey or maple syrup (adjust to taste)
- 8-10 whole cloves
- 2 cinnamon sticks
- 2 star anise
- 1/4 teaspoon ground nutmeg
- Orange zest (from the orange used for slices)
- Additional orange slices and cinnamon sticks for garnish (optional)

Instructions:

Prepare the Ingredients:
- Wash the orange thoroughly and slice it into rounds. Zest the orange to use as a garnish.

Combine Ingredients:
- In a large pot, combine the red wine, orange slices, brandy (if using), honey or maple syrup, whole cloves, cinnamon sticks, star anise, ground nutmeg, and orange zest.

Warm the Mulled Wine:
- Place the pot over medium heat. Warm the mixture slowly, but do not bring it to a boil. Allow it to simmer gently for about 15-20 minutes to infuse the flavors.

Strain and Serve:
- After simmering, strain the mulled wine to remove the spices and orange slices. You can use a fine-mesh sieve or cheesecloth for straining.

Serve Warm:
- Pour the spiced mulled wine into mugs or heatproof glasses. Garnish each serving with additional orange slices and cinnamon sticks if desired.

Enjoy:
- Serve the Spiced Mulled Wine warm and enjoy the cozy and festive flavors.

Tips:

- Adjust Sweetness: Taste the mulled wine and adjust the sweetness by adding more honey or maple syrup if needed.
- Personalize: Feel free to customize the spices to your liking. Some people like to add cardamom, ginger, or a splash of citrusy liqueur.
- Simmer, Don't Boil: Be careful not to let the mulled wine boil, as high heat can cause the alcohol to evaporate.

Spiced Mulled Wine is a delightful beverage that fills your home with warm aromas and is perfect for gatherings or quiet evenings by the fireplace. It's a classic holiday drink that brings comfort and joy to the season.

Holiday Punch

Ingredients:

- 4 cups cranberry juice
- 2 cups orange juice
- 1 cup pineapple juice
- 1 liter ginger ale or club soda, chilled
- 1/4 cup grenadine syrup
- Fresh cranberries and orange slices for garnish
- Ice cubes

Instructions:

Chill Ingredients:
- Make sure all the juices and ginger ale or club soda are well chilled before preparing the punch.

Combine Juices:
- In a large punch bowl or pitcher, combine the cranberry juice, orange juice, and pineapple juice.

Add Grenadine:
- Pour in the grenadine syrup to add a sweet and colorful layer to the punch.

Add Ginger Ale or Club Soda:
- Just before serving, pour in the chilled ginger ale or club soda. The fizz adds a refreshing element to the punch.

Stir Gently:
- Gently stir the ingredients to combine. Be cautious not to stir too vigorously to preserve the carbonation.

Add Ice:
- Add ice cubes to the punch to keep it chilled.

Garnish:
- Garnish the punch with fresh cranberries and orange slices for a festive touch.

Serve:
- Ladle or pour the Holiday Punch into individual glasses and serve immediately.

Optional Additions:

- Alcoholic Version: For an adult version, you can add a splash of vodka, rum, or sparkling wine.
- Cinnamon Sticks: Add a couple of cinnamon sticks to infuse a warm and aromatic flavor.

Tips:

- Make Ahead: You can prepare the juice mixture ahead of time and add the ginger ale or club soda just before serving to maintain its effervescence.
- Customize: Feel free to adjust the ingredient quantities based on your taste preferences.

This Holiday Punch is a delightful and visually appealing drink that can be enjoyed by guests of all ages. It's a great addition to your holiday festivities, providing a burst of flavors that capture the spirit of the season.

Peppermint White Hot Chocolate

Ingredients:

- 4 cups whole milk
- 1 cup white chocolate chips or white chocolate chunks
- 1 teaspoon vanilla extract
- 1/2 teaspoon peppermint extract
- Whipped cream, for garnish
- Crushed candy canes or peppermint candies, for garnish

Instructions:

Heat Milk:
- In a medium-sized saucepan, heat the whole milk over medium heat until it is hot but not boiling. Stir occasionally to prevent the milk from scalding.

Add White Chocolate:
- Add the white chocolate chips or chunks to the hot milk. Stir continuously until the white chocolate is completely melted and the mixture is smooth.

Flavor with Extracts:
- Stir in the vanilla extract and peppermint extract. Adjust the amounts to your taste preference.

Simmer (Optional):
- If you want a stronger peppermint flavor, you can let the mixture simmer gently for a few minutes, but do not let it boil.

Serve:
- Pour the Peppermint White Hot Chocolate into mugs.

Garnish:
- Top each mug with a dollop of whipped cream and sprinkle with crushed candy canes or peppermint candies.

Serve Warm:
- Serve the Peppermint White Hot Chocolate immediately while it's warm and comforting.

Optional Additions:

- Peppermint Syrup: If you have peppermint syrup on hand, you can add a splash to enhance the peppermint flavor.
- Peppermint Schnapps: For an adult version, you can add a splash of peppermint schnapps.

This Peppermint White Hot Chocolate is a delightful treat that's perfect for cozying up by the fireplace during the winter season. The combination of creamy white chocolate and refreshing peppermint creates a comforting and festive drink.

Cranberry Orange Sangria

Ingredients:

- 1 bottle (750 ml) red wine (such as Cabernet Sauvignon or Merlot)
- 1 cup cranberry juice
- 1/2 cup orange liqueur (e.g., triple sec or Grand Marnier)
- 1/4 cup brandy
- 1/4 cup sugar (adjust to taste)
- 1 orange, thinly sliced
- 1 cup fresh cranberries
- 1-2 cinnamon sticks
- 1-2 star anise (optional)
- 1-2 cups sparkling water or club soda (chilled)
- Ice cubes
- Fresh mint leaves for garnish (optional)

Instructions:

Prepare the Fruits:
- Wash the orange thoroughly and slice it into thin rounds. Rinse the fresh cranberries.

Combine Ingredients:
- In a large pitcher, combine the red wine, cranberry juice, orange liqueur, brandy, and sugar. Stir until the sugar is dissolved.

Add Fruits and Spices:
- Add the orange slices, fresh cranberries, cinnamon sticks, and star anise (if using) to the pitcher. Stir to combine.

Chill:
- Refrigerate the sangria for at least 2-4 hours, allowing the flavors to meld. You can also leave it overnight for more intense flavors.

Add Sparkling Water:
- Just before serving, add the chilled sparkling water or club soda to the sangria. Stir gently to combine.

Serve:
- Fill glasses with ice cubes and pour the Cranberry Orange Sangria over the ice.

Garnish:
- Garnish each glass with a sprig of fresh mint if desired.

Enjoy:

- Serve and enjoy this festive and flavorful Cranberry Orange Sangria!

Tips:

- Sweetness: Adjust the amount of sugar to your taste preference. You can start with less and add more if needed.
- Variations: Feel free to customize the sangria with additional fruits such as sliced apples, pomegranate seeds, or berries.

This Cranberry Orange Sangria is a beautiful and vibrant drink that captures the seasonal flavors. It's a wonderful addition to holiday parties and gatherings, bringing a burst of color and festive spirit to your celebrations.

Homemade Eggnog

Ingredients:

- 6 large egg yolks
- 3/4 cup granulated sugar
- 2 cups whole milk
- 1 cup heavy cream
- 1 teaspoon vanilla extract
- 1/2 teaspoon ground nutmeg
- 1/4 teaspoon ground cinnamon
- 1/4 teaspoon salt
- 1/3 cup rum or bourbon (optional, for an adult version)
- Whipped cream and additional nutmeg for garnish (optional)

Instructions:

Separate Eggs:
- In a large mixing bowl, separate the egg yolks from the egg whites. Save the egg whites for another use.

Whisk Egg Yolks with Sugar:
- Whisk the egg yolks together with the sugar in a bowl until the mixture becomes pale and slightly thickened.

Heat Milk and Cream:
- In a saucepan, heat the milk and heavy cream over medium heat until it just begins to simmer. Do not bring it to a boil.

Temper the Eggs:
- Slowly pour a small amount of the warm milk mixture into the egg yolks while whisking constantly. This tempers the eggs and prevents them from scrambling.
- Gradually add the remaining warm milk mixture to the egg yolk mixture, continuing to whisk.

Cook on Low Heat:
- Return the combined mixture to the saucepan and cook over low heat, stirring constantly, until the mixture thickens slightly. It should coat the back of a spoon, and the temperature reaches around 160°F (71°C). This step ensures the eggs are safely cooked.

Add Vanilla and Spices:
- Remove the saucepan from the heat and stir in the vanilla extract, ground nutmeg, ground cinnamon, and salt. Allow the mixture to cool.

Add Rum or Bourbon (Optional):
- If you're making an adult version, stir in the rum or bourbon.

Chill:
- Cover the eggnog mixture and refrigerate it for at least 4 hours or overnight to allow the flavors to meld and for the eggnog to chill thoroughly.

Serve:
- Before serving, give the eggnog a good stir. Optionally, you can top each serving with a dollop of whipped cream and a sprinkle of nutmeg.

Enjoy:
- Serve and enjoy this homemade eggnog with friends and family!

Tips:

- Pasteurized Eggs: If you have concerns about consuming raw eggs, use pasteurized eggs for this recipe.
- Fresh Nutmeg: Grating fresh nutmeg enhances the flavor, but ground nutmeg works well too.

This Homemade Eggnog is a delightful treat that captures the essence of the holiday season. It's perfect for sipping by the fireplace or serving at festive gatherings.

Breakfast/Brunch:

Christmas Morning Casserole

Ingredients:

- 1 pound breakfast sausage (pork or turkey), cooked and crumbled
- 6 slices bacon, cooked and crumbled
- 6 cups cubed bread (French bread or sourdough works well)
- 2 cups shredded cheddar cheese
- 2 cups milk
- 8 large eggs
- 1 teaspoon Dijon mustard
- 1/2 teaspoon salt
- 1/4 teaspoon black pepper
- 1/4 teaspoon onion powder
- 1/4 teaspoon garlic powder
- 1/4 teaspoon dried thyme (optional)
- Chopped green onions or chives for garnish (optional)

Instructions:

Prepare the Casserole Dish:
- Grease a 9x13-inch baking dish.

Layer Ingredients:
- Spread half of the cubed bread in the bottom of the prepared baking dish. Sprinkle half of the cooked sausage, bacon, and shredded cheddar cheese over the bread. Repeat with another layer using the remaining bread, sausage, bacon, and cheese.

Whisk Egg Mixture:
- In a large bowl, whisk together the eggs, milk, Dijon mustard, salt, black pepper, onion powder, garlic powder, and dried thyme (if using).

Pour Egg Mixture:
- Pour the egg mixture evenly over the layered ingredients in the baking dish. Make sure all the bread is soaked in the egg mixture.

Refrigerate Overnight:
- Cover the baking dish with plastic wrap and refrigerate the casserole overnight or for at least 4 hours. This allows the bread to absorb the egg mixture.

Preheat the Oven:
- Preheat your oven to 350°F (175°C).

Bake:
- Remove the casserole from the refrigerator and let it sit at room temperature while the oven preheats. Bake in the preheated oven for 45-55 minutes or until the center is set and the top is golden brown.

Garnish and Serve:
- Optionally, garnish the Christmas Morning Casserole with chopped green onions or chives. Let it rest for a few minutes before slicing and serving.

Tips:

- Customize Ingredients: Feel free to customize the casserole by adding vegetables like bell peppers, onions, or spinach.
- Serve with Condiments: Offer condiments like salsa, hot sauce, or ketchup on the side for extra flavor.

This Christmas Morning Casserole is a crowd-pleaser and a convenient breakfast option, allowing you to spend more time enjoying the holiday with your loved ones.

Gingerbread Pancakes

Ingredients:

- 2 cups all-purpose flour
- 2 tablespoons brown sugar
- 2 teaspoons baking powder
- 1 teaspoon baking soda
- 1/2 teaspoon salt
- 1 teaspoon ground ginger
- 1 teaspoon ground cinnamon
- 1/4 teaspoon ground nutmeg
- 1/4 teaspoon ground cloves
- 2 large eggs
- 1/4 cup molasses
- 1 1/2 cups buttermilk
- 1/4 cup unsalted butter, melted
- Cooking spray or additional butter for greasing the griddle

Instructions:

Preheat the Griddle:
- Preheat a griddle or a non-stick skillet over medium heat. If you're using an electric griddle, set it to 350°F (175°C).

Combine Dry Ingredients:
- In a large mixing bowl, whisk together the flour, brown sugar, baking powder, baking soda, salt, ground ginger, ground cinnamon, ground nutmeg, and ground cloves.

Whisk Wet Ingredients:
- In a separate bowl, whisk together the eggs, molasses, buttermilk, and melted butter.

Combine Wet and Dry Ingredients:
- Pour the wet ingredients into the dry ingredients and gently stir until just combined. Do not overmix; a few lumps are okay.

Grease the Griddle:
- Lightly grease the griddle with cooking spray or butter.

Cook the Pancakes:
- Pour 1/4 cup portions of batter onto the griddle for each pancake. Cook until bubbles form on the surface, and the edges start to look set.

- Flip the pancakes and cook for an additional 1-2 minutes on the other side or until golden brown.

Serve Warm:
- Remove the pancakes from the griddle and keep them warm. Repeat the process with the remaining batter.

Optional Toppings:
- Serve the Gingerbread Pancakes warm with your favorite toppings such as maple syrup, whipped cream, or a dusting of powdered sugar.

Tips:

- Make Ahead: You can mix the dry and wet ingredients separately the night before and combine them in the morning for a quicker breakfast.
- Keep Warm: If making a batch, keep the cooked pancakes warm in a low oven (around 200°F or 95°C) while you finish cooking the rest.

These Gingerbread Pancakes capture the warm and spicy flavors of gingerbread, making them a delicious and festive addition to your holiday breakfast or brunch menu. Enjoy the cozy aroma and delightful taste!

Cranberry Orange Scones

Ingredients:

- 2 cups all-purpose flour
- 1/3 cup granulated sugar
- 1 tablespoon baking powder
- 1/2 teaspoon salt
- 1/2 cup unsalted butter, cold and cut into small pieces
- 1/2 cup dried cranberries
- Zest of 1 orange
- 1/2 cup buttermilk (plus extra for brushing)
- 1 large egg
- 1 teaspoon vanilla extract
- Optional: Coarse sugar for sprinkling on top

Instructions:

Preheat the Oven:
- Preheat your oven to 400°F (200°C). Line a baking sheet with parchment paper.

Combine Dry Ingredients:
- In a large mixing bowl, whisk together the flour, sugar, baking powder, and salt.

Add Cold Butter:
- Add the cold, cubed butter to the dry ingredients. Use a pastry cutter or your fingertips to cut the butter into the flour until the mixture resembles coarse crumbs.

Add Cranberries and Orange Zest:
- Stir in the dried cranberries and orange zest, distributing them evenly throughout the mixture.

Whisk Wet Ingredients:
- In a separate bowl, whisk together the buttermilk, egg, and vanilla extract.

Combine Wet and Dry Ingredients:
- Pour the wet ingredients into the dry ingredients and stir until just combined. Do not overmix.

Shape the Dough:
- Turn the dough out onto a floured surface. Gently knead it a few times until it comes together. Pat or roll the dough into a circle about 1 inch thick.

Cut into Wedges:
- Use a sharp knife to cut the circle into 8 wedges.

Brush with Buttermilk:
- Place the scones on the prepared baking sheet. Brush the tops with a little buttermilk and, if desired, sprinkle with coarse sugar for a sweet crunch.

Bake:
- Bake in the preheated oven for 15-18 minutes or until the scones are golden brown.

Cool:
- Allow the scones to cool on the baking sheet for a few minutes before transferring them to a wire rack to cool completely.

Optional Glaze:
- If desired, you can drizzle the cooled scones with a simple glaze made of powdered sugar mixed with a little orange juice.

Serve:
- Serve these Cranberry Orange Scones with your favorite tea or coffee and enjoy!

These scones are a perfect balance of tart cranberries and zesty orange, making them a delightful addition to your holiday breakfast or brunch table.

Overnight Cinnamon Rolls

Ingredients:

For the Dough:

- 1 cup warm milk (about 110°F or 43°C)
- 2 1/4 teaspoons (1 packet) active dry yeast
- 1/2 cup granulated sugar
- 1/3 cup unsalted butter, melted
- 4 cups all-purpose flour
- 1/2 teaspoon salt
- 2 large eggs

For the Filling:

- 1/2 cup unsalted butter, softened
- 1 cup brown sugar, packed
- 2 tablespoons ground cinnamon

For the Cream Cheese Frosting:

- 1/2 cup cream cheese, softened
- 1/4 cup unsalted butter, softened
- 1 cup powdered sugar
- 1/2 teaspoon vanilla extract
- Pinch of salt

Instructions:

Prepare the Dough:

Activate the Yeast:
- In a small bowl, combine warm milk and active dry yeast. Let it sit for about 5 minutes until it becomes frothy.

Mix the Dough:
- In a large mixing bowl, combine the yeast mixture, melted butter, sugar, salt, and eggs. Gradually add the flour and mix until a dough forms.

Knead the Dough:
- Turn the dough out onto a floured surface and knead for about 5-7 minutes until it becomes smooth and elastic.

First Rise:
- Place the dough in a greased bowl, cover it with a clean kitchen towel, and let it rise in a warm place for 1-2 hours or until it doubles in size.

Prepare the Filling:

Roll out the Dough:
- On a floured surface, roll out the dough into a large rectangle.

Spread Filling:
- Spread the softened butter evenly over the dough. Sprinkle the brown sugar and cinnamon over the butter.

Roll Up the Dough:
- Starting from one of the longer sides, tightly roll up the dough into a log.

Slice into Rolls:
- Cut the rolled dough into 12-15 equal slices.

Arrange in a Pan:
- Place the slices in a greased baking dish, leaving a little space between each roll.

Second Rise (Refrigerate Overnight):
- Cover the baking dish with plastic wrap and refrigerate the rolls overnight for a slow rise.

Bake the Rolls:

Preheat the Oven:
- In the morning, preheat your oven to 350°F (175°C).

Remove from Refrigerator:
- Take the rolls out of the refrigerator and let them come to room temperature as the oven preheats.

Bake:
- Bake the rolls in the preheated oven for 25-30 minutes or until they are golden brown.

Prepare the Frosting:

Make Cream Cheese Frosting:
- While the rolls are baking, prepare the cream cheese frosting by beating together the softened cream cheese, butter, powdered sugar, vanilla extract, and a pinch of salt until smooth.

Frost the Rolls:

- Once the cinnamon rolls are out of the oven and slightly cooled, spread the cream cheese frosting over the top.

Serve Warm:
- Serve the Overnight Cinnamon Rolls warm and enjoy!

These Overnight Cinnamon Rolls are sure to become a favorite for a special breakfast or brunch. The combination of soft, gooey rolls and creamy cream cheese frosting is simply irresistible.

Eggnog French Toast Bake

Ingredients:

For the French Toast Bake:

- 1 loaf French bread, cut into 1-inch cubes
- 2 cups eggnog
- 4 large eggs
- 1/4 cup granulated sugar
- 1 teaspoon vanilla extract
- 1/2 teaspoon ground cinnamon
- 1/4 teaspoon ground nutmeg
- 1/4 teaspoon salt
- 1/2 cup chopped pecans or walnuts (optional)

For the Streusel Topping:

- 1/2 cup all-purpose flour
- 1/2 cup packed brown sugar
- 1/4 cup unsalted butter, softened
- 1/2 teaspoon ground cinnamon
- 1/4 teaspoon ground nutmeg
- Maple syrup for serving

Instructions:

Preheat the Oven:
- Preheat your oven to 350°F (175°C). Grease a 9x13-inch baking dish.

Prepare the French Toast Base:
- Arrange the cubed French bread in the prepared baking dish.

Mix Eggnog Mixture:
- In a mixing bowl, whisk together the eggnog, eggs, sugar, vanilla extract, ground cinnamon, ground nutmeg, and salt.

Pour Over Bread:
- Pour the eggnog mixture evenly over the cubed French bread, ensuring all pieces are coated. Press the bread down slightly to help it soak up the liquid.

Optional Nuts:
- Sprinkle chopped pecans or walnuts over the top if desired.

Prepare Streusel Topping:

- In a separate bowl, combine the flour, brown sugar, softened butter, ground cinnamon, and ground nutmeg. Use a fork or your fingers to mix until crumbly.

Add Streusel Topping:
- Sprinkle the streusel topping evenly over the eggnog-soaked bread.

Refrigerate Overnight:
- Cover the baking dish with plastic wrap and refrigerate the French toast bake overnight, allowing the flavors to meld and the bread to fully absorb the eggnog mixture.

Bake:
- In the morning, preheat the oven to 350°F (175°C). Remove the plastic wrap and bake the French toast for 45-50 minutes or until the top is golden brown and the center is set.

Serve with Maple Syrup:
- Remove from the oven and let it cool for a few minutes. Serve the Eggnog French Toast Bake warm, drizzled with maple syrup.

Optional: Dust with Powdered Sugar:
- For an extra festive touch, you can dust the French toast bake with powdered sugar before serving.

Enjoy:
- Enjoy this delicious and indulgent Eggnog French Toast Bake with your loved ones!

This Eggnog French Toast Bake is a make-ahead breakfast that's perfect for Christmas morning or any holiday brunch. The rich eggnog flavor combined with the crunchy streusel topping makes it a festive and comforting treat.